Do You Need To Make A Financial U-Turn?

Discover the TRUTH about using Bankruptcy to point your finances in the right direction.

By Attorney Christian B. Felden

Food For Thought

In 2013 I helped folks eliminate *$9,912,930* dollars' worth of debt. If you extrapolate that out over my 30+ year career, I'm approaching *$297,387,900* in debt GONE FOR GOOD! No sum is insurmountable!

How much debt can I help eliminate for you?

ISBN:
ISBN-13: 978-1500319656
ISBN-10: 1500319651

Table of Contents

CLIENT TESTIMONIALS:

WHAT SOME OF OUR CLIENTS HAVE TO SAY

Over the course of this book you will see that I absolutely love what I do! My mission is to fight for and guide my clients, with personalized service, through the process of regaining control of their lives after suffering a financial setback – but don't take my word for it, take theirs!

"Thanks so much for everything!!" – Mary Ranck, Florida

"We just want to thank you for all your hard work in helping us with our Bankruptcy. Everyone there has been very courteous and helpful as well as patient. We both appreciate all you have done and will certainly refer anyone we know to you should they need your services." – Charles and Lynn Reber, Florida

"You're my hero!" – S.T., North Carolina

"You have been such a big help. I know you are probably a very busy person and to take the time to speak to me means a lot. May it pay forward. You're my angel!" – Jamie G., Florida

“You’ve been great…do you know that? Really responsive and thorough and always kind. I thank you for that. This has been very overwhelming and embarrassing and you made it much easier than I anticipated.” – Anonymous, North Carolina

“Thank you so much. You are a very kind and understanding individual. More businesses should operate and show compassion as you do.” – Freddie Smiling, North Carolina

I LOOK FORWARD TO SERVING YOU AS WELL!

FAQ: Answers to Your basic Questions

Throughout this book my goals are to both simplify the bankruptcy process and show you just how powerful bankruptcy can be to solve many of the financial problems you may be facing. After reading just the first few chapters of the book you will have a good understanding of the basics of how Chapter 7 Bankruptcy and Chapter 13 Bankruptcy work, and also how the financial problems you are facing can be easily solved.

However, some of you may want a fast answer to a burning question about bankruptcy that is weighing on your mind. Others may be skeptical because you will think it sounds too good to be true, or too easy. You may start off by being skeptical because you've talked to a friend or relative who filed bankruptcy years ago and their experiences don't sound anything like I will describe things in this book.

First, let me assure you that bankruptcy can and does work as easily as I describe it in this book for the vast majority of people. For those of you who want to cut to the chase, let me address the most common questions and concerns I receive from potential clients before going into the basics of bankruptcy and debt.

What can a creditor do to me if I don't file bankruptcy?

Debt collection is a three step process. They can contact you to collect the debt, but they may not make any idle or illegal threats - such as throwing you in jail (remember, debtors prisons went out with the French Revolution); reporting you to social services (no, they can't take your kids); or taking belongings that aren't connected to the debt itself. Some of those things may seem obvious and ridiculous, yet they have all been threatened to clients of mine over the years. Creditors can take you to court and may obtain a judgment against you for the money owed. This judgment lasts for several years (the exact time period varies depending on the state where the judgment is issued). During the time the judgment is valid they may attempt to take your property. This most often involves garnishment of your bank accounts or your wages.

If I ignore my creditors won't they eventually just go away?

This is a more common question than you might think. From a theoretical standpoint you do have three options when you have financial problems. One option you always have is to file bankruptcy. Option two is to work out a deal to pay off your creditors. This second option obviously works for very few people either because they don’t have enough money to work out arrangements with their creditors or their creditors are simply not willing to work with them. The third option is to do nothing. This third option, however, also works for very few people. That's because eventually one or more of your creditors are likely to sue you and get a judgment against you. As mentioned in the preceding section, a judgment is essentially a court order that allows the creditor to confiscate money or assets from you up to the dollar amount of the judgment. This judgment will also last for many years. So where you may not have anything for them to come and take or garnish now, that may not be the case years from now, if you are able to get yourself to a different place financially. Remember, at any point during the life of the judgment the creditor can and will take assets from you even though you may not have owned that asset at the time the judgment was issued. Therefore doing nothing is usually not a reasonable option, unless you're very old, don't have any assets, and are not likely to acquire anymore assets in the future.

TOM'S STORY:

Tom had a unique situation when he first came in to speak with me about filing bankruptcy. He was in a horrible financial state and had been for some time, but he had recently found out that he was coming into a small inheritance that he planned on using to turn his life around. When we parted that day, he ultimately decided to hold off on filing bankruptcy, and tried to pay off his debts with the money he was receiving. Not surprisingly, he didn't receive enough money to pay off all of his debts, so some creditors still went unpaid. He was sued several times and received several judgments for monies he owed, but with no income and no real assets, there wasn't anything for his creditors to take…so he thought. A few years later, Tom, now a successful sales representative, was back in my office signing bankruptcy papers because those judgments didn't go away like he thought they would. I will never forget what he said – he said if, "I had only filed for bankruptcy when I first came to see you, not only would my finances already be cleaned up, but I wouldn't be facing losing over 15% of my monthly income to these sharks. I just can't seem to catch a break!" I reminded him, though, that bankruptcy was the break he needed.

What will bankruptcy do about the collection agencies that keep harassing me?

As soon as your case is filed, the bankruptcy court issues what is called an automatic stay (or stop). The automatic stay is essentially a bankruptcy injunction that forbids your creditors from contacting you or taking any action against you to collect the debt. The federal courts impose strict penalties on creditors for willful violation of the automatic stay, and you may be eligible to receive monetary compensation for these creditor violations.

NANCY'S STORY:

When Nancy first contacted me she was *desperate* to make the noise in her life stop.

She was being harassed non-stop at work, at home, on her cellphone – even her friends were receiving calls from HER creditors looking for payment!

I will never forget the look of relief she had on her face when I told her how the INSTANT her bankruptcy was filed, no one would be able to make threatening calls to her anymore at all hours of the day and night.

The liberation she felt from her nightmare was immediate. She even told me she wasn't afraid to answer her phone anymore, and after seeing her smile, I believe her!

Won't I lose my Retirement Savings if I file for Bankruptcy?

In most states all, or virtually all, retirement account and pension plan funds are exempt from creditors, meaning you get to keep them if you file for Chapter 7 bankruptcy. There are some limitations depending on where you live so you should always remember to ask your bankruptcy attorney this important question. In the states where I practice predominantly my clients are able to protect all of their retirement savings. In Chapter 13 bankruptcy, because your retirement accounts are exempt, they won't affect how much you must repay unsecured creditors.

Marty and Sue's Story:

Marty and Sue were frustrated when they sought bankruptcy advice from me. They had watched their retirement savings dwindle from $80,000 to $40,000 while they tried to pay back creditors who were ruthlessly pursuing collections against them. They never imagined their retirement years would be spent like this, and they certainly never imagined that their retirement account would be depleted so rapidly, with very little progress. I told them to immediately stop the bleeding! By filing bankruptcy, they were able to keep what was left of their nest egg safe, and since retirement accounts are protected in most bankruptcy filings, had they come to me sooner – I could have saved them $40,000 in heartache! Bottom line: Don't allow your financial security to be robbed out from under you!

Plans subject to this exemption include the most common types of pension plans, such as:

- 401(k)s
- 403(b)s
- IRAs (Roth, SEP, and SIMPLE)
- Keoghs
- Profit-sharing plans
- Money purchase plans, and
- Defined-benefit plans.

Although the funds in your retirement accounts may be exempt from creditors, retirement benefits that are paid to you as income are not exempt. For instance, for the purposes of Chapter 13 bankruptcy, this kind of retirement income is included in your repayment plan and will help determine what portion of your unsecured debts you must repay.

Don't I have to give up everything I own if I file for bankruptcy?

Absolutely not! Every state legislature has enacted what are known as exemption laws that protect certain assets from creditors, even if that creditor has a judgment against you. These same exemption laws apply inside bankruptcy as well as outside bankruptcy. Exemption laws vary from state to state. That is why getting advice from a friend who filed bankruptcy in another state often isn't helpful because the exemptions in his or her state are likely to be different than your state. It is important to note that state exemptions laws can also tend to be very generous. Most of our clients who are eligible for Chapter 7 Bankruptcy are able to keep everything they own while completely wiping out their unsecured debt. Determining what assets you can protect is an important step in determining what type of bankruptcy you should file. If you cannot protect everything you own in a Chapter 7, you may decide to file for Chapter 13 Bankruptcy protection instead. Why, you may be asking? Because ***all*** of your assets can be protected in a Chapter 13 Bankruptcy!

I have been told if I file for bankruptcy I will lose my home, is this true?

This is completely false. One of the main purposes for filing bankruptcy is to protect your home from foreclosure. If you are current on your payments, you can protect your home's equity from creditors and keep your home in bankruptcy. As I mentioned in the previous question, state exemptions laws protect certain assets you own and every state has some type of exemption for protecting at least a portion of the equity in your home. For example, the two states I practice in predominantly are North Carolina and Florida. At a minimum, individuals filing for bankruptcy protection in North Carolina can protect $35,000 worth of equity in their primary residence or $70,000 for married couples. This protected equity amount is unlimited for Florida individuals and couples. Plus, as mentioned at the end of the previous section, all of your assets can be protected in a Chapter 13, even excess equity you may have above your homestead exemption limit in those states that have limited homestead exemption laws. *And, as you will learn later in this book when I discuss Chapter 13 Bankruptcies, if you are behind on your mortgage payments, there are options under Chapter 13 Bankruptcy to force your bank to allow you to catch up on your back payments and keep your home - even if it has gone into foreclosure.*

I am married, do both of us have to file bankruptcy?

No. You can file individually. Whether you should or not depends on who is legally liable on the debts that you have, but if you have individual debts then it is safe for you to file individually. However, if you have joint debts with your spouse it is not a good idea to file an individual bankruptcy. The reason I say this is that if only one joint debtor on a joint debt files bankruptcy, the other joint debtor who did not file bankruptcy is still liable for the debt. The nice thing though is that, if you both have to file bankruptcy, a husband and wife can file a joint case for no extra cost. That's like getting two bankruptcies for the price of one.

If I file for bankruptcy, won't everyone know I have filed?

Usually not. While a bankruptcy filing is a public court record, it is not easy for most people to find out about it. It is on a court database that is not searchable from websites like Google or Yahoo. And, unless the person filing for bankruptcy happens to be a celebrity, it is rarely reported in the newspapers. If you are concerned about this, you can check your local newspaper to ensure that it does not report local bankruptcies before we file.

If I filed bankruptcy previously, can I file again?

Yes, but how long you have to wait to re-file depends on the type of bankruptcy that you initially filed and the type of bankruptcy you now wish to file. The time periods vary from two years to eight years.

<u>If I file for Chapter 13 Bankruptcy Relief, will I have to make monthly payments to every creditor?</u>

No. This is why Chapter 13 Bankruptcy is a not a debt consolidation. If you go to a debt consolidation company you may get a minor modification to your monthly payments on your debt, but you will normally end up having to pay all of your creditors back in full. In a Chapter 13 Bankruptcy, your monthly payment is usually based on what you can afford to pay on a monthly basis, regardless of how much unsecured debt you have. So, if your budget shows that you can only afford to pay, for example, $150.00 each month, then that's all you will pay for either three years or five years regardless of if you owe $10,000 or $100,000 to your creditors. You will then pay this amount to the bankruptcy trustee, and he or she will distribute that money to your creditors. At the end of your three to five year bankruptcy plan, any unpaid portion of your dischargeable, unsecured debt (think credit cards, medical bills, personal loans, etc.) is completely wiped out.

TRACY AND DON'S STORY:

Tracy had to drag Don into my office – literally. He was so opposed to the idea of bankruptcy that he could hardly bring himself to speak the word. I reassured him that I was not there to pressure him into any decision, just to lay out his options for him, and he agreed to hear what I had to say. Over the course of our consultation, I found out that Don' didn't feel that they were candidate for bankruptcy because they were still making their minimum monthly payments for their debts. I pointed out that that was great, but were they making any headway on the debt balances themselves? We did the math and quickly came the conclusion that their over $500 a month in minimum payments would take over 50 years to pay back all of their debts! And that was assuming that they could keep up with lofty payments of $500 a month. I did the rough bankruptcy calculations, and based on their income and household size, their Chapter 13 Plan payments would be around $275 per month. That was half of what they were currently paying, AND their debts would be gone (FOR GOOD) in a matter of 5 years. Needless to say, Don realized the gravity of their financial situation at that point and saw the light at the end of the tunnel of debt.

What kinds of debts can I NOT eliminate under bankruptcy?

You cannot eliminate student loans, certain tax debts, or court ordered support payments. You also cannot eliminate some debts incurred within 60 to 90 days of filing for bankruptcy (Such as purposely running up your credit card debt right before filing bankruptcy). You typically cannot eliminate secured debts (such as mortgages or car loans) for personal and real property that you plan on keeping. However, as you will learn later, in many cases you can modify payments on car loans.

What about the companies I see on TV that say they will wipe out my debts without bankruptcy?

To this I say, be afraid – be very afraid. There are many unfounded claims being made by agencies that do not have the right to practice law. The Federal Trade Commission recently warned of these "credit repair" scams. The truth is, these companies depend on your creditors voluntarily agreeing to reduce your debt in exchange for your lump sum payment. Unlike legal debt relief, they cannot force your creditors to stop harassing you or even to participate in the deal. They cannot stop collection agency harassment or judgments against you. Only legal debt relief through bankruptcy can. Furthermore, they usually charge far more to reduce a few of your debts than any attorney charges to legally eliminate *all* of the same debts in bankruptcy.

Do I have to make a court appearance?

Usually no. The only appearance the vast majority of bankruptcy filers make is at an informal 341 Creditor's Meeting where there is no judge. The bankruptcy trustee will ask you a few questions for the record about your bankruptcy at this meeting. These questions usually take less than 5 minutes to complete.

If I file bankruptcy, won't my credit be messed up for 10 years?

If you file, the bankruptcy is allowed to remain on your credit report for up to 10 years, however, this does not mean that you cannot get credit during this time period. It simply means that it is allowed to remain on your credit report for this period of time. How long it takes you to obtain credit will really depend more on the other circumstances going on in your life at the time you apply for credit than it will on the bankruptcy. Most lenders these days will do a full review of your credit request despite the bankruptcy on your record. If you have a good cash flow and steady income situation, you will probably not find it difficult to obtain most types of credit right away. Also, as of the time of your bankruptcy discharge, you will have a fresh start to rebuild your credit with no debt burden. The alternative to not filing bankruptcy is to go on with debts hovering over you that will take many years to pay off, and will remain on your credit report for 7 years after that - usually an even worse situation than bankruptcy. This is especially true with judgments which may be collected for many years after they are placed against you. It is typically far worse to have a judgment on your record than a bankruptcy.

If I file for bankruptcy, what happens to my credit score?

There is no doubt that your credit score will go down as a result of a bankruptcy filing, but your credit score is only one component that lenders use in determining your credit worthiness. Lenders also look at your income and your debt burden. If you have missed payments, have collection accounts, have judgments, or repossessions, your credit score is already very low. Bankruptcy will lower the score even more, but bankruptcy can also eliminate your debt burden completely. In a lender's eyes, this can make you more credit worthy since your income is free from the burden of your old debt payments. Moreover, once you make a fresh start, you will be able to rebuild your credit over time.

INTRODUCTION

If you're reading this I would like to extend to you two very different sentiments by way of greeting: Congratulations and I'm so very sorry.

Congratulations because you are brave enough to realize that you have a significant financial problem, and you realize that you need to do something about it – now. You want to thoroughly review all of your options before making what could be one of the most important financial decisions of your life, and I applaud you for that courage.

I'm so very sorry though, because you *do* have a substantial financial problem - whether of your own doing, because of someone else, or simply because you are a victim of circumstances - and you feel that bankruptcy could be an option for you at this time in your life.

The year 2014 marks the 31st year that I have been representing bankruptcy clients, most of those within the states of Florida and North Carolina. Don't worry if you are reading this from somewhere else. Fortunately, bankruptcy law is federal law, not state law, and although some aspects of state law do apply, in general the principles outlined in this book are accurate wherever you happen to live.

Let me start off by saying that, in the 31 years I've been representing folks in bankruptcy court, I've never met anyone who actually wanted to file bankruptcy. Bankruptcy is just not one of those things you do because you want to do it, and certainly no one expects to have to file bankruptcy, but it sure is nice to be able to use its protections if you need to. That being said, I'll tell you exactly what I say to all of my potential bankruptcy clients: I automatically assume that I am the last person you feel like talking to, and I'm ok with that. You wouldn't be human if you weren't feeling those feelings. These days lawyers overall are not high in popularity polls to begin with but, as a bankruptcy attorney, I have to deal with that along with the added fact that I am usually meeting people who are under a great deal of stress and pressure, and are usually at their wits end.

People are usually at one of the lowest points, if not the lowest point, in their lives when they turn to me for advice. For me though, it's this last part that makes it all worthwhile. Counseling people at one of their lowest points and being able to give them the means to claim their lives back is why I love my job. I can be the guiding light in giving people back their hope and, if you want my personal opinion, that is about as rewarding as it gets in the life of a lawyer. There's nothing like watching the stress visibly lift off of those sitting across from me at my desk as I explain to them how easy it is for them to resolve their financial problems. And it is easy for you to resolve your financial problems too. I've outlined the steps to making a financial U-turn with the principles in this book. And I'm guessing that right about now you feel like you need to take a U-turn in your life.

You may be wondering, why write this book? After all, with technology and the internet there's certainly plenty of information about bankruptcy available to anyone at the click of a mouse. That's undoubtedly true. Perhaps it's easiest to explain my reasoning by telling you who this book is ***not*** written for. I did not intend this book for the legal scholar or law school student looking for a technical analysis of the bankruptcy laws. There is plenty of that sort of information readily available on the internet. Instead, this book is written for those of you who don't know the first thing about what bankruptcy is, or how it can work for you. This is for those of you seeking information from a place of completely stressed out, ashamed, helpless, hopeless confusion. Maybe you've done a little research online only to find the information overwhelming, contradictory and basically just a bit scary.

I'm here to present the information to you in plain English. My most sincere hope is that by the time you finish this book you will see that there is a way for you to start over whether you are 18 years of age or 98 years of age – and that no amount of debt is too big to overcome. Remember, your current circumstances do not have to be a permanent prediction of your future. The bankruptcy solutions to your financial problems – whether they be debt, foreclosures, repossessions, garnishments, etc. - are much simpler and easier than you might expect.

So let's get started!

CHAPTER ONE: THE BASICS OF DEBT

Step one: take a deep breath and try to relax. This may sound hokey, but as complicated as you feel your financial situation is, the solution to the problem is usually very simple and straightforward. There are two basic reasons for this: The first reason is that your direct financial stress is most likely caused by simply not having enough money to go around. The good news here is that bankruptcy takes care of your cash flow problems immediately by taking care of your debt situation immediately. The second reason, and perhaps the more significant reason for the simplicity of the solution to your problem, is the fact that for the vast majority of consumers, all of your debt will fall into one of four basic categories under bankruptcy law. So to recap: bankruptcy will free up some of your money immediately, and you really only have up to four types of debts. Seems easier already, doesn't it? Before we start talking about the different types of bankruptcies available to you, let's work to understand these four different types of debts better.

The most common categories of debt are:

1. Priority Debts
2. Secured Debts
3. Unsecured Debts
4. Student Loans

Each of these are treated a bit differently depending on the type of bankruptcy you file. By taking a closer look at these four debt categories, you will begin to see where they might fit into your personal financial situation.

1. **Priority Debts** – You probably have never heard of a debt described as a "priority debt" before, and that's because this is a category of debt uniquely created by the bankruptcy laws and doesn't actually exist outside of bankruptcy law. So what are the bankruptcy laws considering a priority debt anyway? The most common types of priority debts you will have are income taxes and divorce related debts, such as alimony and/or child support. Why are these classified as priority debts? That's a good question with several different reasonable answers. Probably the easiest to understand though, is this line of reasoning: Congress, who enacted

the Federal Bankruptcy Laws, wanted to protect both itself (tax debts) and those who depend upon support for the health and welfare of themselves and their children (alimony and child support). The significance of these being priority debts is that you will not be able to get rid of them in bankruptcy, but you still may be able to get assistance in paying them off under more favorable terms than you normally would outside of bankruptcy.

2. **Secured Debts** - These types of debts are pretty common and you will recognize the two most prevalent types right away: mortgages and car loans. A secured debt is a type of debt where you've pledged something as collateral for repayment of the debt. For example, when you bought your car or your home, you signed two important documents. The first was the promissory note. This is the "IOU" document. It is the promise or obligation to repay the money you borrowed from the bank or other financial institution. The second document that you signed was a mortgage (in the case of a home purchase), or a security agreement (in the case of the car purchase). This mortgage or security agreement gives the bank the right to foreclose on your house or repossess your car in the event that you do not comply with the

terms of the promissory note (the most common type of non-compliance of course being missed payments), the "IOU". Secured creditors are generally protected in bankruptcy to the extent that they either have to get paid something, or else you have to give them back the collateral. You may be surprised to learn though that, bankruptcy isn't always about just getting rid of debt. Sometimes it's about restructuring debt and lowering payments. Even though you generally cannot get rid of secured debts like the ones mentioned above, there are many occasions when you can use your bankruptcy to help you to catch up on payments on your mortgage or car loan, and even lower your car payments. We will discuss these benefits further in Chapters 3 and 4.

3. **Unsecured Debts** - This is a very large category of debts and includes just about everything that we haven't talked about already, with the exception of student loans. The statistics for American credit card debt alone in 2014 was a household average of $15,191.00. So we can draw the conclusion that almost everyone has some of this type of debt. This is the category that includes credit cards, medical bills, payday loans, personal loans, and old utilities bills, such as cellphones, electric, rent,

etc. Having too much of this type of debt is probably the most common cause for people to file for bankruptcy. But this is the category of debt that is most exciting to deal with in terms of bankruptcy because this is the easiest type of debt to get rid of in any type of bankruptcy case!

4. **Student Loans** - This category of debt requires no explanation. If you're in college, or if you have attended college in the not too distant past, chances are that you have some student loan debt. Unfortunately, as with priority debts, you can't get rid of student loan debt in bankruptcy (except under *very* limited and extreme circumstances). However, all is not lost. You may be able to get some cash flow relief in bankruptcy from this type of debt by deferring payments on student loans for up to five years.

That pretty much sums up the basics of debt and what the specific categories of debt are in bankruptcy. Now let's see how they all fit within the bankruptcy process.

Chapter Two: Chapter 7 and Chapter 13 in Plain English

Since we are now going to start talking about bankruptcy itself you might anticipate this to be the largest part of this book. However, remember what I told you earlier - I didn't write this book for attorneys, law students, or anyone else looking for the technical aspects of bankruptcy. I wrote this book for the normal person who doesn't care about a technical legal analysis of the law, but rather is more concerned about their real world problems and how bankruptcy can help them deal with the types of debts and financial problems that they are facing at this moment in time. Your initial concerns are probably more aligned with knowing whether you're going to lose your house, your cars, your retirement accounts, or whatever other assets you may own. I will, of course, get to the answers to all of those questions in due time. In fact, as you'll see in the later sections of this book, I will address each of these issues and assets directly. But before I get to the basics of Chapter 7 and Chapter 13 Bankruptcy, or answering your pressing questions about what the bankruptcy means to the assets you have worked so hard to accumulate, let me first answer the question that I probably get most of all: *Yes, you do qualify for bankruptcy!* I don't know where this idea originated, but most people are under the impression that that there are all sorts of requirements that need to be met in order for someone to qualify to file bankruptcy, or even to be considered bankrupt for that matter. This is simply not true. In fact, I would be so bold as to say that everybody, at every stage of their life qualifies for at least one type of bankruptcy. The only real question is what type, or types, do you qualify for, and which one might be better for you under your particular circumstances. You may find it surprising, but it is rare for a bankruptcy trustee or other bankruptcy official to even ask you why you're filing bankruptcy in the first place, or how you got in the condition you're in. The reason for this is simple - it just doesn't matter. It matters greatly to you of course, but to the bankruptcy court these particulars are not important to the case. So, whether your current financial mess is your own fault, someone else's fault, or you're just a victim of circumstances, you qualify.

Now that we have gotten the qualifications for bankruptcy out of the way, are you ready for my version of the "detailed technical analysis" of the two most common types of consumer bankruptcies, Chapter 7 and Chapter 13? Okay, here we go.

Chapter 7 Bankruptcy - These types of bankruptcies are what we refer to as liquidation type bankruptcies. Chapter 7's are asset based, and typically are the type of bankruptcy that you might consider filing if you have limited income, limited assets, and have no special circumstances. Why? Because you need to make below a certain income level to file this type of bankruptcy. You can also potentially lose assets if you own too many. I commonly refer to Chapter 7's as "plain vanilla" type bankruptcies. They are great at getting rid of unsecured debts, but not much good for anything else. If you have lots of credit card bills and/or medical bills, have limited income, and own limited amounts of assets, the Chapter 7 Bankruptcy could be a perfect fit for you. An added benefit to this type of bankruptcy is that they are fast and, for many people, practically over the day you file the case.

Chapter 13 Bankruptcy - These types of bankruptcies are what we refer to as reorganization type bankruptcies. They are not to be confused with debt consolidations. Let me repeat that: THEY ARE NOT TO BE CONFUSED WITH DEBT CONSOLIDATIONS! This is a common misconception about Chapter 13 cases - that they are just debt consolidations where you end up paying everyone back. That is false. In Chapter 13 cases you get rid of debts just like you do in any other type of bankruptcy case. Chapter 13's are simply a more comprehensive approach to bankruptcy, because in Chapter 13 cases not only can you get rid of certain types of debts, but you can restructure other types of debts, and defer debts as well - all wrapped up in one nice, neat little package. So, if too much unsecured debt is just one part of your financial problem, and you may also be facing a foreclosure on your home, or a potential car repossession, or you simply have too much student loan debt that you can't afford to pay it back right now, a Chapter 13 Bankruptcy could be the answer to all of your financial problems.

That's it. That was my not-so-technical, technical analysis of your common bankruptcy filings. Let's get to the things that you care about the most, and find out how bankruptcy can help you solve every single one of the financial problems that you face. How does a clean start sound to you?

Chapter Three: Yes, You Can Keep Your Home ...and Here's How

As the title to this chapter plainly states, yes, you can keep your home. But there is an important stipulation to this statement: you can keep your home, *as long as you can afford to keep paying the mortgage*. Keeping your home is a very common concern for those who come to see me for bankruptcy help. With the unfortunate downturn in the real estate and job markets over the last several years, it's become all too common of a concern. There is hope though for those of you with homes, and it doesn't matter if you are current or behind on your mortgage payments. As mentioned in previous chapters, people typically think of bankruptcy as something that only gets rid of debts. This, of course, is true, but when it comes to homes and mortgages the bankruptcy process provides different strategies altogether that help you keep your home, and give you time to get caught up on past due payments.

Let's look at the common types of situations homeowners are faced with when they consider bankruptcy. One of these scenarios will probably look a lot like yours:

1. You are up-to-date on your mortgage payments;
2. You are behind on your mortgage payments;
3. You are behind on your real estate taxes or homeowners associations dues;
4. You own a home that has decreased substantially in value;
5. You own your home free and clear.

Homeowners Who Are Up-To-Date On Their Mortgage Payments

I start off with this group of homeowners because this one is the easiest. If you fit into this category, then it's real easy to keep your home when you file bankruptcy. Just keep making your mortgage payments like you always have....nothing changes.

Homeowners Who Are Behind On Their Mortgage Payments

You may think that if you fit into this category of homeowners that all hope is lost and there is no way that you can keep your home. Perhaps the bank may already be in the process of foreclosing on your home as you are reading this. Well, the good news for you is that one of the unique things that you can do in a Chapter 13 Bankruptcy case is cure defaults in secured loans like mortgages. What does this mean to you? You can force your creditor (bank) to allow you to get caught up over time, without the constant threat that you will be thrown out of your own home. How it works is very simple: No matter how far behind you are on your mortgage payments, on the day you file a Chapter 13 Bankruptcy, (whether you're one month behind, two months behind, 10 months behind, or 5 years behind), for all practical purposes your mortgage is treated as if it were in good standing again.

Once your bankruptcy is filed, you start making your regular mortgage payments to the bank, just like you always had, and the bank is obligated to accept them. You then catch up on all of the back payments on your mortgage through your bankruptcy plan over a three to five year time period. This a very powerful bankruptcy strategy which is used by many homeowners to keep their homes. To summarize the importance of this strategy one again, in a Chapter 13 Bankruptcy case you can stop the bank from foreclosing (or even think about foreclosing if they haven't started the process yet) on your home; force the bank to reinstate your mortgage; force the bank to start accepting your regular monthly mortgage payments again; and force the bank to give you up to five years to catch up on any missed mortgage payments without additional late fees, additional penalties or additional interest accruing. WOW!!! The only thing you cannot do in bankruptcy is force the bank to modify your regular monthly mortgage payment. That is why I mentioned the stipulation before that you can keep your home as long as you are able to make your regular monthly mortgage payment. You are, however, allowed to pursue a separate loan modification while you are in an ongoing bankruptcy.

Homeowners Who Are Behind On Their Real Estate Taxes or Homeowners Associations Dues

I listed this as a separate category because these situations represent two additional ways that you can lose your home that not everyone thinks about. If you don't pay your real estate taxes the county can sell your home at a tax sale. Additionally, if you live in a neighborhood with a homeowner's association, very often the association's by-laws provide that the homeowner's association can foreclose on your home, just like a bank, if you don't pay your association dues. As you can imagine, these situations, although they can happen independently, are often joined together with a default in mortgage payments. The connection with mortgage defaults doesn't end there though. As with falling behind on your mortgage payments, in a Chapter 13 Bankruptcy case you can also cure a default in your real estate taxes or homeowner's association dues, much in the same way that you can get caught up on your mortgage arrearage. You can force the taxing authority or homeowner's association to give you up to five years to catch up on any missed payments through your Chapter 13 reorganization plan, without the constant threat of foreclosure.

Homeowners Who's Homes Have Decreased Substantially in Value

In Chapter 2 where I discussed the different types of debts, I mentioned to you that secured creditors normally are protected in bankruptcy to the extent that they usually have to get paid something or you have to return their collateral. As with most things in bankruptcy however, there are certain exceptions to the general rules. The meltdown in the real estate market that began in late 2006 to early 2007 presented a unique situation that rarely had to be addressed years ago, but was becoming more and more commonplace: homes were decreasing in value, one, two and three times over. While this state of affairs has become less frequent with the recent stabilization of the real estate market, we bankruptcy attorneys are still seeing this situation come into our offices on a fairly regular basis. So what happens when the home that you love and want to keep has decreased in value substantially? I am not talking about a mild decrease, which most people have experienced in recent years, but a substantial decrease to the point that your home is now worth *less* than what is actually owed on the first mortgage. What is the significance in bankruptcy if this has happened to you? Nothing if you only have one mortgage on your property. However, if you are like many people who have second

GERRY'S STORY:

Gerry came to me with one goal in mind – to keep the home he loved. Between the unbelievable downturn in the real estate market in Florida and a recent divorce, he was finding himself farther and farther behind on his payments. He could meet the first mortgage obligations every month but not the second or the third, and he couldn't see any solution that didn't end in his losing his home. In a nutshell, he had already lost so much of the life he once had, he was despairingly trying to find a way to not lose this too. We did a market analysis on his home and soon found out that it wasn't worth even what was owed on the first mortgage anymore – normally not good news to have to stomach hearing, but in a bankruptcy situation, this is great news! I was able to help him get rid of the second and third mortgages from his home, allowing him to keep the property and making it more affordable for him, and I was able to help him clear up the other debts he had been left with in the wake of his divorce! Gerry's life may be different now, but it is without a doubt a good different.

mortgages, third mortgages or home equity loans, then the significance can be great. If you have a home that is now worth less than what you owe on your first mortgage, you can get rid of the secondary mortgages altogether in a Chapter 13 Bankruptcy case. To be clear, in order for this to be possible, the value of your home *must be less* than what you owe on your first mortgage alone. The theory behind this is that if your home is worth less than what you owe on your first mortgage, then there really isn't any equity in your home protecting your second mortgage company anyway. Thus, the second mortgage, which on paper appears to be a secured loan, really is unsecured and, in a Chapter 13, you can essentially change it to unsecured debt and get rid of it just like any other unsecured debt. That means you can keep your house and only be obligated to pay back what is owed on your first mortgage. This could be a savings of many hundreds of thousands of dollars for you!

Homeowners Who Own Their Homes Free and Clear

This is a category that is more common than you might think, and I feel that it is worth mentioning to put your mind at ease. What happens if you own your home free and clear, but by all other standards you are bankrupt, and you are afraid that filing for the protection you need means you will lose your home?

I won't keep you in suspense and give you the quick answer. There is no reason for you to lose your home in bankruptcy. How you can protect it even under these circumstances depends in part on where you live and in part on what type of bankruptcy you file. Earlier I mentioned to you that each state has laws known as exemption laws that protect certain assets in bankruptcy. These exemptions laws differ from state to state, but every state has a homestead exemption that protects at least some of the equity in your home. In many states the amount of the homestead exemption is enough to protect all of the equity in your home. In those states where the homestead exemption is not enough to protect all of the equity in your home you can still protect the remaining equity in a Chapter 13 case. That's because in Chapter 13 cases you can prevent the loss of any of your assets. This means that you can keep your home, even if you own it free and clear, and still be able to get the relief you need from other creditors by filing for bankruptcy.

Now let's turn our focus to another cherished asset that most people have, your vehicle.

Chapter Four: You Can Keep Your Car ... And Maybe For Less than You Are Paying Right Now

Next to losing your home, the second biggest concern that most people have when they come to visit me for bankruptcy counseling is that of losing their car. As before, I am pleased to tell you that there is no reason for you to lose your car when you file bankruptcy. In fact, the different bankruptcy strategies available to you with regard to cars, often times, makes the car more affordable as well. That means that the car you were considering letting go of (because you didn't think you could afford to keep up with the high monthly payments anymore), may become affordable again thanks to your filing for bankruptcy relief. Just like we did with homes, let's look at the most common situations that you may face as a car owner at the time you file bankruptcy:

1. You have owned your car for less than a year and are <u>current</u> on your car loan payments;
2. You have owned your car for less than a year and are <u>behind</u> on your car loan payments;

3. You have owned your car for more than a year, but less than 910 days (approximately 2 ½ years);
4. You have owned your car for more than 910 days, and the car is worth less than what you owe on the loan.

Car Owners Who Have Owned Their Cars for Less Than a Year and are Current on Their Payments

Just like those of you with mortgages who are current on your mortgage payments, I start off the automobile section with car owners who are current with their car payments because they are treated much the same in bankruptcy. The only difference is that I added the condition that you must have had your car financing in place for less than a year. You'll see why the year matters in the following sections. The good news again here is that there's no reason for you to lose your car when you are in bankruptcy. For those of you who have owned your car for less than a year and are current on your car payments, keep making those payments on time directly to the auto financing company just like you always have, and nothing changes.

Car Owners Who Have Owned Their Cars for Less Than a Year and are Behind on Their Payments

Here is your situation: You are behind on your car payments, you have owned your car for less than a year, and the bank is most likely threatening repossession. What can you do? The good news in this scenario is that as long as you can afford to make the car payment, you can keep your car. Plus, just like the situation where you are behind on your mortgage payments, you can use a Chapter 13 Bankruptcy to force the auto financing company to give you up to five years to catch up on any back payments that you owe.

Before we move onto the next section, I'd like to add a comment because you might think that the first two sections are great in the way you get to keep your car and catch up on your payments if you are behind. However, the real magic of a Chapter 13 Bankruptcy case comes into play when you've owned your car for more than a year. How would you like to restructure your car loan and lower your interest rate? How about lowering your monthly payment altogether? What about lowering the remaining balance on the loan itself? You'll see how a Chapter 13 filing can help you accomplish these things in the next two sections.

<u>Car owners who have owned their car for more than a year but less than 910 days (approximately 2 ½ years)</u>

Let's start off this section with a simple example: A car owner has owned his car for about a year and a half. He has a $22,000.00 balance remaining on his car loan, which is financed at an interest rate of 7.5%. His current monthly car payment is $525.00. With me so far? So what can a Chapter 13 Bankruptcy do for this car owner? I hinted at the answer earlier with my side note. One of the unique things that you can do in a Chapter 13 Bankruptcy case is restructure automobile loans. In the current example this car owner can lower his interest rate from 7.5% to 5.25%, and then restructure his loan by extending it out another full five years through his Chapter 13 reorganization plan. Is he current or behind on his car payments? It doesn't matter. That's correct, it doesn't matter. This is a bankruptcy rule that can benefit both car owners who are current or behind – as long as you have owned the vehicle for at least a year. You may be asking, why would he want to take advantage of this if he is current? Well, by using this part of the bankruptcy code, he is able to lower his car payments to $418.00 per month. That's a $107 per month savings, before he eliminates any other debts he may have. Sounds pretty good right?

Let's try another set of numbers, so you can have an estimate of what you may be able to lower your car payment to: If you owe $10,000 on your car, your new car payment could be under $170 per month after filing for Chapter 13 Bankruptcy! If you owe $30,000 on your car, your new car payment could be reduced to $500 per month after filing for Chapter 13 Bankruptcy! You get the picture – this equals big savings in your pocket! And remember, if you are a car owner who is behind on his or her payments, you wouldn't have to worry about catching up at all in this scenario. The payments would be absorbed into the new restructured loan.

Car Owners Who Have Owned Their Car for More than 910 Days and Their Car Value is Less Than the Balance on Their Car Loan.

In this section we get to see even more of the magic of a Chapter 13 Bankruptcy. By adding only two more facts to the examples from the previous section, what seemed like a pretty good thing, can get even better. Take a look: In this example, the car owner has had his car and financing in place for more than 910 days. The *value* of his car is only $9,000.00, not the $22,000 that is outstanding on his loan. Sounds pretty familiar, right? Nothing depreciates quite as quickly as a vehicle. So what additional benefits could there possibly be in a Chapter 13 with these different facts? Well, we could reduce his car payment to around $150.00. If you remember from the previous section, his current car payment is $525 per month. That means, since the *value* of his car is less than the outstanding loan, that he could save $375 per month on his car payment alone. See what I mean when I say that applying the bankruptcy laws to your individual situation can relieve an enormous financial burden from you immediately?!?

How this can be accomplished in Chapter 13 Bankruptcy is very simple. In a Chapter 13 Bankruptcy case, if you've had the financing in place on your car for more than 910 days, <u>and</u> your car is worth less than what you currently owe on it, you can reduce the amount you owe on your car to the value of the car itself. In other words, it wouldn't matter if the balance on your car loan was $10,000.00 or $22,000.00 or $50,000. In either instance, it's only the value of your car that is important and, if it's only worth $9,000.00, that's all you have to pay back to the creditor in order to own your vehicle free and clear. The balance of the loan is eliminated in the bankruptcy much like any other unsecured debt. Pretty spectacular if you ask me!

As you can see from these examples, not only can you keep your car in bankruptcy, but in many cases you can use the bankruptcy to make your car payment more affordable, and free up some cash so you can breathe easier on a monthly basis right away.

MELISSA'S STORY:

In one 72 hour period Melissa went from working at her dream job and living a life that seemed like it could only go up, to losing her job and facing having her car repossessed in the dark of night in the not too distant future. It started when she went to cash her paycheck on Friday, and the check wouldn't clear. By Monday she was boxing up her desk along with over half of her co-workers, wondering how she was going to feed her son, pay the rent and provide a mode of transportation for them. Unfortunately, hard times hit even the largest employers and Melissa's company was being downsized – a lot. She came to see me after finding temporary work (thank God!), but with a dilemma – she was still two months behind on her car payments because she couldn't come up with that large of a sum monthly anymore. She had owned the car for a few years and didn't feel like the balance was ever going to go away. We took a look at the numbers, and because the vehicle had some years on it, it wasn't worth nearly as much as she still owed. When we filed her bankruptcy, not only could she now sleep soundly though the night not having to worry that the car would be taken while they were sleeping, but we were able to decrease her payments by over half of what she was paying. Now she knew that she would be able to get her son to the school bus every morning, get herself to work every day and she will own her car free and clear in just 3 years time. She also was able to get rid of the minimal credit card debt that she had accumulated while she was out of work, and break the cycle of constant stress that had become her normal day to day life.

CHAPTER 5: MAKING A FINANCIAL U-TURN

Let's face it – we all know this scenario a little too well. It's late, you're driving on a road you aren't very familiar with and you suddenly realize that you are not headed in the direction that you want to be going. You may have made a wrong turn, you may have followed some form of wrong directions or you may just be riding shotgun in the front seat, but we have all been there. You need to make a U-turn and try to find your way back to where you want to be heading.

The same is true of bankruptcy. Think of it as making a U-turn in life. As I mentioned before, you may be in this financial mess because of something that you personally did, something that someone else did to you, or you may very well just have been in the wrong place at the wrong time… but isn't it nice to know that you can make a U-turn with your financial life as well? Isn't it nice to know that you don't have to face your future with all of the burdens of your past mistakes? I would be lying if I told you that I hadn't made many of those mistakes, or failures actually, myself. It is human nature. You cannot succeed in this life without failing every now and then, because, really, it is all part of the game we call life. You win some and you crash and burn on others. Luckily, most of life's decisions turn out to be good ones – or else we would all be functioning like pre-programed robots on a daily basis… but there are always those choices every now and again that make us sit back and just say, "Man, I really messed up this time. How did I ever end up here?" But much like the scenario of being in that car, lost, eventually we do find our way to where we want to go, and I firmly believe that bankruptcy can help to turn around all of the past financial mishaps that you have. I have seen it happen time and time again as I guide my clients through the process.

Close your eyes and imagine for a moment – ok, don't close your eyes, because you would have a hard time reading this page – but imagine for a moment, a time when you could open up the mailbox, and be happy about what you were receiving, not petrified to open that letter and find out how much debt you were in now, or what your neighbors might think if they saw all of the obnoxious collections notices poking out of your mailbox. Imagine not having your telephone ring hundreds of times a week with calls from nasty, low life collectors who threaten to take everything from your home, including your children and pets; but instead being excited to hear who was calling you to chat or share great news from their day. Remember that time when the sound of a telephone didn't cause a lump in your chest and a knot in your stomach? Or better yet, imagine sitting down to put together your budget and actually having money left over at the end of your month, rather than month left at the end of your money.

Mistakes happen. Failure happens. Debt happens. Part of what makes us who we are is our ability to make choices for, and to think for, ourselves. I hope that you will think about what can be gained from making a U-turn with your finances, and choose to give yourself a break. Give yourself a break from all the pressure you feel yourself under right now. Give yourself a break from the suffocating stress that you feel on a day to day basis. Give yourself a break for making a bad decision, or two, or ten. It happens. It's human. It can be fixed.

In closing, I will leave you with this thought:

"A wrong path doesn't make a permanent destination. You can always change your direction. Don't let anyone ever tell you you're forever lost."

– Dodinsky

Let's turn it around – together!

The Bible and Bankruptcy: A Biblical Connection to the Modern Bankruptcy Code And Overcoming the Moral Dilemma

As I mentioned very early on in this book, I don't think I have ever met anyone who actually wanted to file bankruptcy. I will say though, that everyone I have filed bankruptcy for has ultimately come to the conclusion that it was the last hope they had of getting out of financial trouble and getting back on their feet again. For some of these people it is simply the right thing to do financially and for others it is purely a business decision. For many though, the decision to file bankruptcy is both gut wrenching and provides a moral dilemma. This chapter is written for those of you who are wrestling with the moral aspects of filing for bankruptcy protection.

Many people conduct themselves from a standpoint that places primary importance on faith, trust, and obedience to God. As such, when you find yourself contemplating bankruptcy, or find yourself in a situation where you will be unable to honor the financial obligations that you have agreed to and are obligated to pay, it is understandable that where one's personal faith in God is concerned, it may seem like there would be a conflict with the legal remedies available to you as a struggling debtor, resulting in your hesitancy to file for bankruptcy relief.

The Bankruptcy Code was designed to provide U.S. consumers relief from seemingly insurmountable amounts of debt. Many are unaware, however, that the Bankruptcy Code and a number of its constituent elements, were in part conceived around Old Testament or Torah concepts found in the Bible. In fact Christian or Jewish adherents to the Old Testament might recall God ordering the release of debtors from their obligations every seven years.

The Christian Bible and the Jewish Torah in the Book of **Deuteronomy 15:1-2**, state this divine proclamation of periodic release from debt in the following way:

> ***1At the end of every seven years thou shalt make a release. 2And this is the manner of the release: Every creditor that lendeth ought unto his neighbour shall release it; he shall not exact it of his neighbour, or of his brother; because it is called the LORD's release.***

We find also in the Book of **Nehemiah 10:31**, reference to the standard practice of periodic debt forgiveness in biblical Jewish culture:

> ***...and that we would leave the seventh year, and the exaction of every debt.***

Modern considerations toward exempting a worker's "tools of the trade" from taking in the bankruptcy process, among other examples, are also present in the Bible in **Deuteronomy 24:6**:

> ***No man shall take the mill or the upper millstone to pledge: for he taketh a man's life to pledge.".***

Other instances of mandated periodic debt forgiveness, laws against usury, and forgiving the debts of the impoverished are also present in the Holy books of our nation's major faith groups.

Ultimately, when it comes to interpreting the laws of God and man, people need to come to their own conclusions, or consult trusted resources when considering the discharge of debts, or entering into debt relief plans under the US Bankruptcy Code. For many of my clients over the years who have struggled with the moral aspects of bankruptcy, I have tried to ease their dilemma by explaining an aspect of bankruptcy that they may not understand: When you receive a discharge from the Bankruptcy Judge, that is a final order that prevents most of your creditors from ever doing anything to ever collect money from you again for that debt. There is nothing, however, in the Bankruptcy Code that prevents you from voluntarily paying back anybody you want to in the future, if you are able. Therefore, if you find yourself in a financial position in the future that would allow you to pay your creditors back and ease any moral dilemma you may still have, you are free to do so.

Made in the USA
Middletown, DE
19 January 2025

68936983R00038